WARREN BUFFETT

AN ILLUSTRATED
BIOGRAPHY OF
THE WORLD'S
MOST
SUCCESSFUL
INVESTOR

A COMIC BY AYANO MORIO

WARREN BUFFETT

AN ILLUSTRATED
BIOGRAPHY OF
THE WORLD'S
MOST
SUCCESSFUL
INVESTOR

A COMIC BY **A**YANO **M**ORIO
TRANSLATED BY **M**ARK **S**CHREIBER

John Wiley & Sons (Asia) Pte Ltd

Manga Warren Buffett
Copyright © 2003, Ayano Mario. All rights reserved.
English translation published by arrangement with
John Wiley & Sons (Asia) Pte Ltd through Panrolling, Inc.

This edition published in 2005 by John Wiley & Sons (Asia) Pte Ltd
2 Clementi Loop, #02-01, Singapore 129809

This publication is designed to provide accurate and authoritative information with regard
to the subject matter covered. It is sold with the understanding that the Publisher is not
engaged in rendering professional services. If professional advice or other expert assistance
is required, the services of a competent professional person should be sought.

Other Wiley Editorial Offices

John Wiley & Sons, Inc., 111 River Street, Hoboken, NJ 07030, USA
John Wiley & Sons Ltd, The Atrium, Southern Gate, Chichester PO19 BSQ, England
John Wiley & Sons (Canada) Ltd, 22 Worcester Road, Rexdale, Ontario M9W ILI, Canada
John Wiley & Sons Australia Ltd, 33 Park Road (PO Box 1226), Milton, Queensland 4046, Australia
Wiley-VCH, Pappelallee 3, 69469 Weinheim, Germany

Library of Congress Cataloging-in-Publication Data:

0-470-82153-1

Typeset in 9-18 point, Comic Sans MS and ComicsCarToon by Red Planet
Printed in Singapore by Saik Wah Press Pte Ltd
10 9 8 7 6 5 4 3 2

TABLE OF CONTENTS

BUFFETT'S RULES FOR SUCCESS

1929: The Wall Street Crash

Soon, capital pours out of equities into government bonds; businesses everywhere collapse and millions are out of work...

Into the family of a struggling Mid Western stockbroker, a baby is born.

He is to become the most successful investor of all time: **Warren Buffett.**

Growing up during the Depression had a profound effect on Warren Buffett.

Warren was born on August 30, 1930.

Don't cry, Warrie.

His father, Howard, sold securities for a bank. When it collapsed, he lost everything.

The Depression got worse and worse. Throughout the Midwest, farmers were going broke.

Howard set up his own stock-broking firm, hoping for better times.

Chapter 1 Getting Started

After five long years of hardship, things improved for the Buffetts, and they moved into a better house.

But Warren never forgot the pain. Everyone knew he wanted to get very, very rich.

Many years later, a young man travels to Omaha. He wants to discover how Buffett achieved his dream.

Excuse me, sir.

Could you tell me where Warren Buffett lives?

Sure! Right over there.

Huh?

That place?

That's just an ordinary middle-class home.

I've known him since he was a kid. He's just a regular guy.

Can you tell me about him?

How does he do it?

Really?

He doesn't have a big organization - I heard he only has about ten employees-and a normal-looking office. Nothing special.

How does he compete with those big Wall Street firms with thousands of employees?

What does he do that they don't?

Warren Buffett is pretty special, you know. He's very, very smart. And honest.

If you stick around awhile, you'll get the idea.

See that?

Here's your paper, sir.

Thanks a lot.

That's right – Warren Buffett started with a paper route, didn't he?

Sure did. At the age of 13.

Morning.

Hi there.

You're gonna leave them there?

They're too heavy, so I split them into two piles and leave them on the 8th and 4th floors. Then I work from the top floor down.

Smart kid.

CLATTER

JANITOR

Excuse me.

I have to collect subscriptions tomorrow. Can I leave the envelopes with you?

Sure. I'll pick up the money as people go out.

Hey, kid. I want to cancel the **Washington Post** beginning next month.

Yes, ma'am.

Rats! One less customer.

Maybe she's just changing to another paper. I'd better start handling the **Times Herald** too.

KNOCK KNOCK

201

Dareca San

CLACK
CLACK
CLACK

Are you thinking of switching to the **Times Herald?**

I deliver that too, now.

Hello, ma'am. I know you're cancelling the **Washington Post.**

Well...

You're a sharp kid. OK, I'll take the Herald.

That's how he got his deliveries up to 500 customers a day. Then he started delivering magazines.

By the time he was 14, he was earning $175 a week – as much as the average 25 year-old was earning.

That's amazing.

7

Say, could I get you a drink? What'll you have?

SCREECH!

Okay, I'll have a coke.

That's what Warren Buffett drinks, isn't it?

He used to drink Pepsi, but he switched to Coke when he bought the stock.

Coca Cola!

Get your Coca Cola!

When he was 6?

That'll be 5 cents, please.

He started selling Coke at 5 cents a bottle when he was 6 years old.

He'd buy a 6 bottle pack for 25 cents and sell them in the neighborhood.

I make 5 cents per half a dozen bottles. That's just over 16% gross profit.

He must have been a strange kid.

Not that strange... but he loved numbers. Everyone knew he was smart. And he's conservative, too. He says he only invests in businesses he can understand.

I guess he understood Coca Cola pretty well by the time he bought its stock.

Does he time the market?

Not exactly. He's big on value. He doesn't like to invest unless he thinks that a company is cheap.

He likes a bargain.

9

If he thinks that a company is worth more as a business than it's selling for in the stock market, then he says it is cheap.

Cheap? What's cheap about Coca Cola?

That might just be because the market is down.

Have you studied his methods?

Well, not really...

Okay, the first thing you should do is read **The Intelligent Investor** by Benjamin Graham. That's what got Buffett started.

BOOK STORE

Here it is.

The Intelligent Investor
by Benjamin Graham

There's a preface by Warren Buffett.

I read the first edition of this book in early 1950...

In his preface Buffett recommends Chapters 8 and 20 as the most important.

...We are convinced that the average investor cannot deal successfully with price movements by endeavoring to forecast them....

This is amazing.

Wow!

To the 19 year-old Buffett, **The Intelligent Investor** was an inspiration.

For years he had been searching for a systematic approach to stock picking.

Graham's ideas made sense. He argued that a company has a value in the real world as a business. Sometimes the market overvalues it, and the stock price is high. At other times, the market undervalues it, and the stock price is low.

Eureka!

According to Graham, all an investor has to do is to buy companies at a lower price than their "true" value, subject to certain stringent tests. Sooner or later, the price will rise.

Graham was not interested in what companies actually did. All he wanted to know was what they were really worth.

Through detailed analysis, an investor can discover the true value...

This is amazing. Why hasn't anyone else thought of this?

Most books about the market focus on predicting price trends.

Warren reads through the night.

Dawn breaks...

BENJAMIN GRAHAM

In 1934 Benjamin Graham and a former assistant, David Dodd, published a book called **Security Analysis**. This massive volume helped to establish stock and bond analysis as a professional discipline. After World War Two Graham decided to write a shorter version for the benefit of non-professional investors: **The Intelligent Investor**.

Benjamin Graham's approach is known as "value investing". It is a simple idea: if you buy a company's stock for less than its per share net asset value, you have bought a bargain.

But a $1 book value bought for 40c is still only worth 40c in the market. Graham believed that over time the stock price would tend to adjust towards the book value, enabling you to make a profit.

Graham's investment business barely survived the Depression and he never forgot the hard times. For this reason, he had very stringent criteria for stock picking, including:

* Industrial firms should have current assets worth at least twice their current liabilities. Long-term debt should not exceed working capital.

* The stock should have paid dividends for the last 20 years.

* The company should have "a minimum increase of at least one-third in per-share earnings in the past ten years using three-year averages at the beginning and end."

* The current stock price should not be more than 15 times the last three years' average earnings.

* The current stock price should not be more than 1.5 times the last reported book value.

Using these rules, a portfolio would consist of unpopular, unpromising stocks with low capitalization. To Graham, this didn't matter - these stocks are "cigar butts" that someone has thrown away, but you can still get a few good puffs out of them by holding them for a few years.

CHAPTER 2 MEETING BENJAMIN GRAHAM

After two frustrating years at the Wharton Business School, Buffett completes his degree in Nebraska. Then he enrolls at Columbia, where Benjamin Graham teaches stock analysis part time.

Yes?

There's something I don't understand.

Say I find an undervalued stock and invest, how can I be sure that the price will eventually rise?

What's the mechanism? Why should the market adjust at all?

Look, the market may take an inconveniently long time to adjust to a rational valuation.

I don't know what the mechanism is, but I can tell you that in my experience it usually does readjust eventually.

So the market is rational sometimes.

Sure. But it is like a manic-depressive most of the time,

alternating between extremes of optimism and pessimism. The investors' advantage is that they can choose when to sell. To do that well, you need to master these principles:

1 Investigate.

2 Do everything possible to determine that your valuation is correct.

3 Determine whether the company has appeal

Your assignment this week is to analyse the accounts of a real company.

See if you can guess its name.

In the library...

Benjamin Graham is the chairman of GEICO, an insurance company based in Washington.

Warren decides to check it out...

There it is!

GEICO

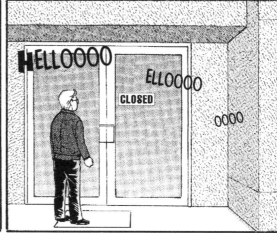

HELLO! HELLO? ANYONE THERE?

BANG BANG BANG BANG

CLOSED

Hold your horses. I'm coming.

Do you work for GEICO?

No, I'm the janitor.

I came all the way from New York. Is there anyone in the GEICO offices?

I think there's someone up on the 6th floor...

I'm sorry to bother you. I'm studying with your chairman, Professor Graham, at Columbia. I just wanted to learn more about the company.

Uh... hello?

Who's that?

Professor Graham?

Yes, Benjamin Graham. I've been analysing GEICO's intrinsic value, and I want to check if my conclusions are correct. Could you help me?

Let's take a look. My name's Lorimer Davidson, by the way.

Davidson spends
four hours
with Buffett.

Davidson is
vice-president
of finance.
He later becomes
GEICO's COO.

This kid
really
knows his
stuff.

Mr. Davidson was a
really nice man.
He took a lot of trouble
to answer my
questions
carefully.

WOW...

WOW!

The future value of GEICO is five times its current stock price.

Its sales costs are much lower than its competitors' and it specializes in low-risk customers.

Buffett visits a Wall Street insurance analyst.

So you don't think GEICO is great value?

It's too expensive. I'd want to see the price drop substan -tially.

All over
Wall Street,
Buffett hears
the same story.

This is great.
None of the
analysts
see GEICO's
true value.

They're just looking
at price trends.

Benjamin Graham's
a genius!
He's the first man
to take a scientific
approach
to stockpicking.

Warren took 2/3rds of his savings

— $10,000 —

and bought GEICO stock.

A year later, he sold for $15,000
— a profit of 50%.

As graduation approaches, Warren starts thinking about his future.

Professor Graham, could I ask you something? It's important.

Would you give me a job at your firm? I'll work for free, just to get the experience.

Gee, Warren...

I need to talk to my partner.

You're my best student ever, Warren. But there are other things to consider.

A few days later...

I'm very sorry, Warren, but there aren't any openings for you at Graham-Newman.

* A long time later Warren discovered the reason for the rejection. Most Wall Street firms discriminated against Jews; as a Jewish firm, Graham-Newman had a policy of positive discrimination. While Warren had a chance to work for any Wall Street firm, many young Jews had few opportunities to work in finance.

Sigh

I thought he liked me...

As Graham's top student, Warren had been certain he'd get the job.
The shock hit him hard.

Warren returns to Omaha after graduation. He meets a girl...

Hi, Susie!

You wanna go for a soda?

Sure, Warrie.

How come you're so crazy about stocks?

They're a great way to make money. If you know what you're doing.

The more I get to know you, the stranger you seem...

Yeah, I guess.

Ya know, Susie, what really makes me tick is the fear of dying. I don't believe we go anywhere when we die... so I don't wanna die.

You know I was so sick when I was little? I really suffered. I've been thinking about death my entire life.

You're not scared?

No, Warren, I'm not.

And you don't have to be, either.

Oh, Susie, you dreamboat.

You want me to show you some great stock picks? You'll make a buncha dough.

Uh, I'll take a raincheck, Warren.

Look at the time...

See ya.

I've gotta go — I have a date.

Sigh

Of course she has a date.

Who'd want to go out with a dufus like me?

31

But...

She's
the only one
for me...

I'll bide
my time.

Maybe
she'll
come
around.

Susie's
house.

I think
I'll go
and say hi
to her
parents.

A ukulele! That's Susie's Dad playing.

Hi, Mr. Thomson.

Would you like to try a duet?

That's great, Warren.

Every evening Warren goes to play the ukulele with Susie's dad, a prominent Presbyterian minister.

You guys are improving.

Are you going out again?

I have a date, Dad.

Why don't you stay in some time and eat with us? And Warren here.

33

You know, Warren is a really fine young man.

You shouldn't be put off by his modesty.

It's a virtue.

Gee, Dad really does like him...

And he hates my other boyfriends.

Sure, Dad, let's all have dinner together some time.

Susie was an obedient girl.

And Warren had been working to improve his charm.

Warren's so smart. And I feel sorry for him.

All those pent-up emotions and complexes. I can help him.

Spring, 1952.

Warren and Susie get married. Susie is only 19.

Married life...

Gosh, this apartment is such a dump. And Warren scrimps and saves so hard...

I don't know what we'll do when the baby comes along.

Warren goes to work at his father's small stockbroking firm, selling securities. He isn't exactly a born salesman.

I'll check them out with some of my more experienced advisors.

Thanks for the tips, son.

But... But...

DRRING! DRRRINNGGGG!

Honey, it's Benjamin Graham on the phone.

Huh?

He called!

37

Warren joins Graham-Newman as an analyst. The firm operates a mutual fund that only invests in very cheap stocks. It ain't all roses....

Sir, I know this one doesn't meet all your usual tests, but look! It's trading at $45 and has $120 per share in cash at the bank!

No.

It fails on several points.

I don't need to take the risk.

Okie-dokie.

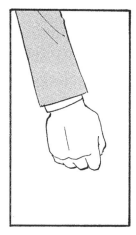

Rats.

Warren starts investing his own money in the stocks Graham rejects. He makes money. Life at Graham-Newman becomes frustrating.

40

CHAPTER 3 DISCOVERING INTANGIBLE VALUE; THE AMEX AFFAIR

After Graham-Newman closed, Buffett quickly organizes a limited partnership for family and friends - they give him $105,000 to invest. He puts his own money into a separate partnership. Shortly afterwards, a fan of Benjamin Graham gives him $120,000 to manage. Buffett is now running three limited partnerships from his bedroom in Omaha. Other investors follow. By 1961, he has millions under management, and has massively outperformed the Dow Jones Industrial Average:

	DJIA	Buffett
5-year cumulative gains	74.3%	251%

What's this?

oils in food pro- dies to... ... In a previous trial, a judg...
ast year but that
llion pounds (250
or 4 percent, were
s.
Sumichrast, an
and publisher of a
n newsletter, said
y could well repeat
million pounds (300
) a year, down from
d 1.6 billion pounds
on kg) in the mid-

ree consecutive de-
shed activity down to
nally adjusted annual
$413.5 billion.
y assurance'' seal for
nd vegetables to grow-

the Malaysian Palm Oil
Growers Council has mounted
an information campaign and
has underwritten medical stu-
dies to support its case.   judge

been linked with high blood
cholesterol levels and heart
United States may average
about 1.84 billion pounds (840
million kg) since 1985, but the
portion used in food products
February decline rep-

eral recomme...
intake of dietary
cially saturated fat
stant film and came
booted Kodak out
stant photography
saddling it with $600
...ses and an estim...

AMEX POSTS $1.5 BN LOSS. FRAUD DISCOVERED IN SUBSIDIARY

Amex is a great company. Maybe this is an opportunity.

Hey, Warren. Long time no see.

Oh, hi! How's business?

Same ol', same ol'.

Uh huh

What are you looking at, Warren?

I'm watching your cash desk.

A lot of customers are using credit cards to pay.

Yeah, people love 'em.

They don't seem to be worried about the Amex scandal.

Okie-dokie!

SLAM

Buffett goes all over town, watching how shoppers pay. Then he visits Amex's competitors.

You wanna know what I think?

That was real helpful. So long.

I'm glad Amex has a problem. It gives the rest of us a chance to gain market share. They've been top dog for too long.

Back to study Amex's numbers...

Sales at Amex have grown continuously for ten years. What a great business!

Warren decides that Amex has a strong franchise and a near-monopoly in its market. Benjamin Graham only used "tangible" assets, like buildings and machinery, in his valuations. Buffett decides that an "intangible" franchise has an intrinsic value too. He invests 25% of his assets in Amex.
Not long after...

What?

Amex stockholders are suing the president!

They want to stop him from compensating the victims of the fraud.

Hi, Mr. Clark.

As a substantial investor, Buffett gets a meeting with the president of Amex.

I fully support what you are doing. You are right to compensate those people,

...even if you could wriggle out of it. I'll help you in any way I can.

Mr. Buffett, I appreciate this.

We need all the support we can get right now.

Buffett agrees to testify in court.

I believe that stockholders should support Mr. Clark's principled stand, not only for moral reasons but also because it is good business. Amex may not be legally responsible for its subsidiary's liabilities in this matter, but by acting generously it will restore its reputation as a fine American company. Mr. Clark has offered $60 million in settlement. It's really not a large sum.

45

The lawsuits drag on, but the Amex stock price begins to rise.

Mr. Buffett, congratulations. Your Amex play has really paid off.

It was the negative media coverage that hurt the stock price.

Amex got so cheap I had to buy it.

How did you know things would improve?

It's a really good business - it is growing well and enjoys a near-monopoly in its market. It was never going to collapse.

BUFFETT'S RULE FOR SUCCESS No 1

ASCERTAIN THE TRUE QUALITY OF A COMPANY AND ITS TOP MANAGERS.

Around this time, an investor invites Warren to lunch.

Warren, I want you to meet Charles Munger. I think you have a lot in common.

I don't believe it.

Hi.

He looks like me.

We could be twins.

What's your racket, Warren?

We have a partnership. I'm interested in investing for value.

From what I hear, you have performed extremely well.

We do ok.

Hey, if that's okay, I'm in the wrong business. Maybe I should give up law and do what you do.

Yeah, maybe you could.

Warren and Charlie hit it off immediately. Charlie is just as smart as Warren, but more talkative. It's a true meeting of the minds.

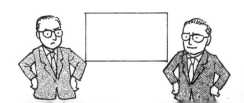

48

CHAPTER 4 THE WARREN AND CHARLIE SHOW

Buffett has been intellectually isolated for too long, and hates to discuss his stock picks with anyone until the action is all over. But with Charlie, things are different. He needs someone to talk over his ideas with.

Soon, he and Charlie are talking on the phone every day.

Warren, this company Berkshire Hathaway. What were you thinking? It makes suit-liners - are you nuts? Where's the future in that?

It's a value play, Charlie. It has more than $2 of working capital for every $1 in its stock price

You may get stuck with it, Warren.

Either that or I'll sell out at a profit. But I think I could turn it around.

Buffett is moving away from Graham's ideas about buying cheap companies. Maybe a good price for a great business was better than a great price for a lousy business... Nevertheless, Berkshire Hathaway is a classic Grahamite play. It's cheap, but it doesn't have a rosy future.

It's clear that Berkshire's business is in trouble...

Mr. Buffett, this is Stanley Rubin. I'm a vice-president at Berkshire Hathaway.

May I ask you what your plans are for the company? Do you intend to buy more stock?

I hear you already have a substantial holding through nominees. Is this is a takeover play? Why don't you come out to Massachusetts to see us?

Well, possibly.

I'd be glad to.

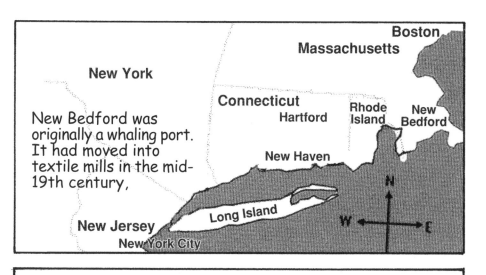

New Bedford was originally a whaling port. It had moved into textile mills in the mid-19th century,

The industry slowly began to contract in the early 20th century. By the early 1950s, Berkshire Hathaway was the dominant player in a shrinking game.

By the time Buffett came along, Berkshire's 12,000 workers had shrunk to 2,300 and its assets had fallen by half.

How do you justify this continual investment in machinery? What makes your products better than the competition?

Berkshire has made losses for 8 consecutive years.

What is being done about it?

53

Ken Chace does his best to answer all the questions. It isn't easy.

I have to be frank, Mr. Buffett.

I don't believe that the board is facing up to these problems. Something radical is needed.

But I don't see any sign of it happening...

Do you think they will listen to reason?

To be honest, no.

Meanwhile, in the president's office...

There's a fund manager snooping around the plant. I don't like it. Who does he think he is?

My son is going take over this firm!

I'm not going to let any Wall Street slicker interfere.

I'll buy back that man's stock.*

A few days later...

So they want to buy back the stock.

Warren has a chance to sell out at a profit.

I guess I'll sell if the price is right.

Hmmm

SHUFFLE

SHUFFLE

But I can't help thinking...

* By buying back Buffett's stock with company money, the number of shares in issue would be reduced. The president would increase the proportion of stock under his control, thereby making it harder for anyone to mount a hostile takeover.

Buffett decides to approach some of the other major stockholders to see if they will sell out to him. If he can acquire enough stock, he'll control the company...

Here it is

Buffet arranges a meeting with the company's chairman.

CREAK!

By coincidence, the chairman has the same surname as the executive who showed him around the plant - Chace.

I'm sorry Mr. Buffett, I won't sell to you.

But some of my associates may be willing to do so.

Thank you for your frankness. Mr Chace.

I appreciate it.

Word gets around quickly in New Bedford...

Mr. Buffett, I'd like to sell you my stock.

That's great. Do you know anyone else

who will do the same?

Ken Chace gets a call...

Ken? It's Stanley Rubin. Buffett wants to meet with you.

swivel

swivel

Hiya, Ken! Good to see you again.

Don't look so surprised. You wanna popsicle?

Uh, thanks.

Here, take it.

Ken, how would you like to be president of Berkshire Hathaway?

GULP

I now control enough stock to push your appointment through, if you'll accept.

But please keep this confidential.

I'd be honoured, Mr Buffett

Ken, I want you to start planning exactly how you are going to put the company back on its feet.

And you had better start writing your first speech as president.

Dazed

Well, see you at the next board meeting.

I'll take that wrapper.

Uh, thanks.

The meeting lasted just ten minutes...

...but I think he means what he says.

Next, Buffett approaches the current president's younger brother, Otis, another major stockholder.

Buffett's a strange fellow...

60

Buffett and Stanley Rubin discuss tactics before the meeting.

I don't foresee any problems.

Here he is now.

CREEAAK!

Mr Stanton, if you sell me your stock, I will have a controlling interest in the company. I propose to make Ken Chace president in place of your brother.

Huh?

Do we have a deal?

On one condition - that you offer my brother the same price for his stock that you're offering me.

Agreed. Can I count on your support at the next board meeting?

I don't think my brother has the stomach for a real fight...

It's for the best.

Please understand that I only want what's best for the company.

It's about time someone took control.

Yes.

BUFFETT'S RULE FOR SUCCESS No 2

STOCKHOLDERS ARE NOT MANAGERS.
THEY SHOULD LEAVE THE RUNNING OF A FIRM TO
COMPETENT MANAGERS WITH INTEGRITY.

Armed with 49% of the stock, Buffett pushes his agenda through...

With Ken Chace in charge, the company became more efficient. It even started making profits. The stock price climbs...

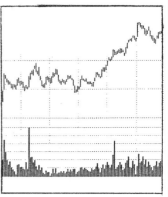

Buffett plans his next move...

Knock, knock

Come in.

What would it take for you to sell?

GRIND

The only people who have tried to buy me out have been crooks and deadbeats

It sounds like you have some conditions

I wouldn't want any of my staff to lose their jobs. The other stockholders should get the same price that I get if they sell.

Anything else?

I want the company to stay in Omaha.

Do you have any other conditions?

Isn't that enough? No one wants to accept my terms.

Well, do you have a price in mind?

GNASH

The market price is $33. I want $50 per share.

Well...

Jack, I accept all your terms. You have a deal.

Huh?

...and the other stockholders get 50 bucks a share too. That's fine.

GIGGLE

Now, you did understand all the terms, didn't you, son? No job cuts, no move from Omaha...

Uh?. Okay, we have a deal

The deal took 15 minutes, and Berkshire Hathaway bought its first insurance company.

The insurance business is unusual in that it takes large sums of cash upfront, in the form of premium payments, but only has to pay out in the event of a claim.

The fund of premiums is called the "float". Under Nebraska's loose regulations, insurance companies could invest their float more actively than in other jurisdictions. By buying National Indemnity, Buffett had access to a stream of cash for investment.

CHAPTER 5 BUFFETT DISSOLVES THE PARTNERSHIPS

By 1966 the stock market was overheating, driven in part by the production-boosting war in Vietnam. Electronics, conglomerates and "growth" stocks were in fashion, and

new mutual funds were opening every day. Fearful of a crash, Buffett decides to close his funds to new investors. A year passes, and stocks just keep going up.

KNOCK KNOCK

Hi Warren. I want to talk to you.

Sure. What's on your mind?

I've invested with you for years, as you know, and you have done a great job.
But the market's changed. You've got to get into these electronic stocks.

They're the future! These new fund managers really get technology — and their returns have been amazing recently.

My brother just made 10 times his money in under a year.

You are hiding your head in the sand, Warren.

People are getting rich out there!

I know that some investors have made out like bandits lately. And that some professional fund managers have outperformed our partnerships lately.

But I have to tell you, these technology businesses don't make any sense to me.

They look way, way overpriced.

I invest in businesses I understand. Investments that are popular are not necessarily good investments,

so I try to ignore what the Wall Street crowd is doing.

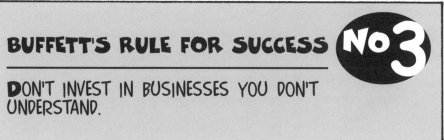

BUFFETT'S RULE FOR SUCCESS No3

DON'T INVEST IN BUSINESSES YOU DON'T UNDERSTAND.

On Wall Street, people started running Buffett down. His conservatism now looked like pigheadedness

In the brave new world of "synergies" and "innovation"

Buffett was looking... kind of square

The market is way too high...

...but I can't prove it...

THAT'S IT!

SCRAPE

I'll quit!

I can't beat these gamblers in the short term.

I'll give my investors their money back.

In 1969, Buffett dissolves the partnerships. His personal wealth is now $10 million. He's only 39 years old.

I am not attuned to this market environment and I don't want to spoil a decent record by trying to play a game I don't understand...

His partnerships now have assets of $105 million. He sells most of the stock and distributes the cash.

Buffett gives his investors the option to keep stock in two companies, Berkshire and Diversified Retailing. He tells them to invest with Bill Ruane's Sequoia Fund if they want to stay in the market. But he recommends that they put their money into municipal bonds His timing is immaculate. By the end of 1969, the stock market is way down.

CHAPTER 6 SEE'S CANDIES

Warren!

Hey, Charlie.

Enjoying your retirement?

Have you read Phil Fisher's book?

Common Stock and Uncommon Profits. Yeah.

I like how he researches growth companies. He really gets his hands dirty.

Does all the researc himself.

Talks to everyone in the industry, hears all the rumours.

1971. Although Warren and Charlie call each other every day - sometimes every hour - they keep their businesses separate. Charlie operates his own fund out in Los Angeles. By coincidence, they both start investing heavily in Blue Chip, a trading stamp company that collects a fee from supermarkets in return for supplying trading stamps that are given to shoppers. When shoppers have collected enough stamps, they can redeem them for items such as toasters and garden furniture.

Charlie and Warren like Blue Chip for the same reason: it collects its fees up front, but only has to pay out for its gifts much later. In the meantime, it has a big float of money - and unlike insurance companies, there are no rules on how this money must be invested.

Warren becomes the biggest stockholder in Blue Chip and Charlie the second biggest.

Let's see, these discounted cashflow figures don't look quite right. What if I adjust...

DRRING
DRRINGG

Warren? It's Bob Flaherty here. I'm sitting with Bill Ramsey of Blue Chip,

and we have a live one.

We want you to buy See's Candy.

You have heard of the company, I guess.

Gee, Bob.

I don't think we want to be in the candy business...

CLICK!

What happened? Lisa, the phone went dead. Get me Warren Buffet again, please.

Maybe he hung up. Maybe he just hates candy.

He's such a strange guy — you can't tell what he's thinking.

After a few minutes, Bob gets through again.

Warren?

Bob, I've just been looking at See's numbers. I'm interested.

Huh?

74

I only want it at the right price, though. How much do they want?

$30 million

That's a little steep. Their book value is $25 million. I'd buy it for that much. Can you fix up a meeting?

Sure.

See's Candy was a long-established family firm manufacturing premium boxed candies, mainly fancy chocolates.

It sold these exclusively through its own chain of 200 stores.

Hmmm... See's is a very seasonal business. Most of their sales are in the two months before Christmas.

The brand name is clearly valuable. But what is it really worth? Can we add value to the brand?

The following year, Buffett buys See's for $25 million. He makes few changes...

Just keep making candy the way you always have. We want everyone to know that See's Candy is the best in America.

That's not a problem.

Buffett starts learning about sugar futures. If See's can get the best prices on the sugar it uses, it can substantially enhance its profits.

If we can cut costs and raise prices, this will really work.

Charlie, I've been thinking. Isn't it great to control really healthy businesses? I'm sick of turnaround situations.

Warren realizes that he enjoys having a controlling interest in the companies he invests in — and he doesn't want to sell them for a quick profit.

Sure, Warren but what if they can't expand?

Then we focus on efficiency!

BUFFETT'S REVISED RULES FOR SUCCESS

1 Pick companies that are simple to understand.

2 Pick companies with stable long-term performance.

3 Pick companies that have a promising future.

I'm thinking more and more like a businessman and less and less like a stockmarket trader. I want established concerns with very strong market position, so that they can control their prices. I'll try to avoid heavily regulated industries...

Buffett's activities at Blue Chip eventually got him into trouble with the Securities and Exchange Commission (SEC). He was investing actively on behalf of three different entities: Berkshire Hathaway, Diversified Retail, and Blue Chip Stamps, each with a different set of stockholders.

Buffett tried to act fairly, but a conflict of interest arose; through Blue Chip, he made a small investment in Wesco Financial, a savings and loan company. When Wesco announced a merger, Buffett and Munger bought more stock in an attempt to prevent it, and became Wesco's biggest stockholders, with 24.9%.

In 1974 the SEC began to investigate Buffett's actions, accusing him of manipulating Wesco's stock price. For two long years, the SEC ground down on him, demanding thousands of documents and endless explanations.

Eventually the SEC accepted that Buffett had only committed minor technical infractions and the case was settled for a small penalty. The nightmare was over.

Buffett quickly rationalized his companies by consolidating Wesco within Blue Chip and merging Diversified Retailing with Berkshire Hathaway.

From then on, Berkshire Hathaway became the parent company for all Buffett's holdings.

CHAPTER 7 A PLATONIC AFFAIR...

In 1963 the president of **The Washington Post**, one of America's major daily newspapers, committed suicide.

SHRIEEEEK!!!

His widow, Katharine Graham, is a highly-educated socialite with no business experience. She decides to take over the leadership of the news-paper.

That's no job for a woman....

She's has no right to tell us what to do...

Her colleagues gave her a hard time.

In 1973...

CLICK

Mrs. Graham!

I've found out who's been buying up our stock. It's an eccentric hayseed from the Bible Belt. I'm very concerned that he may want to interfere editorially.

He's acquired 0% of the stock?

We can't allow some ambitious fund manager from Nebraska to tell us what to do!

Hmmm

But our advisors tells us that the family owns all the voting shares.

He can only buy the B shares, and they don't have voting rights.

I don't understand stocks. Maybe he could do some damage.

We've got to keep people like this away from the paper!

I agree.

81

Here it is! I knew the name sounded familiar.

But I can't remember anything about him.

Hello, Bob.

Say, I need some information.

What do you know about Warren Buffett?

Katharine asks Wall Street acquaintances about Buffett. They warn her to be careful.

Warren writes to her, telling her about how he delivered the Post as a school kid.

This man doesn't seem like a menace. This is a really nice letter. I'd better meet him.

Mrs. Graham?

As I mentioned in my letter, delivering the Post was one of my first ventures into business.

Your paper, sir!

I'm investing in your company for the long term. It's always been a part of me, and I'd like to get closer.

Hmmm.

Is this guy for real?

It takes a long time for Katharine Graham to trust Warren, but eventually she invites him onto the board.

Buffett loves the excitement of being around an important newspaper. As he gains Katharine's confidence, he begins to give her a few hints on how to improve the business.

Every time he comes to Washington, Warren spends time talking to Katharine about finance and the stockmarket.

Some of her colleagues are suspicious, but she likes his style.

So if the Post buys back its stock in the market...

...earnings per share improves.

Soon, Katharine is using Warren's financial terminology at meetings with other executives. A lot of people think he has too much influence over her.

His influence grows:

- **T**he pressroom at the Post is grossly overstaffed, thanks to a powerful union. Katharine takes them on, causing a bitter strike. During the four-month battle, she relies on Buffett to warn her if the struggle is becoming too damaging in financial terms. With his support, the union is finally defeated.

- **T**ime Inc., owners of the Washington Star, offers a deal to share the combined profits of both newspapers. Buffett persuades Katharine to nix the deal - and the Star goes out of business, leaving the Washington Post with the entire market.

- **O**ver the next decade, earnings per share go up ten times, thanks to the stock buybacks.

Katharine has things to teach Warren, too:

- **S**he takes him to VIP dinners, where he mixes with Washington's rich and powerful.

- **S**he teaches him how to eat gourmet food - although she can't persuade him to stop drinking Coke.

- **S**lowly, she persuades him to improve his wardrobe and deportment.

People start to wonder if Warren and Katharine are having an affair — even his kids are confused. But the relationship is platonic — they really are "just good friends."

85

CHAPTER 8 THE RETURN TO GEICO

Warren had fond memories of GEICO, the insurance company he had visited in Washington when he was Benjamin Graham's student.

Over the years, GEICO had grown to become one of America's largest auto insurers.

In 1976,

GEICO posts a loss of $126 million

Kodak had violated seven of Polaroid's key patents on in- of fats and oils in food prod- ucts in the last year but that only 550 million pounds (250 million kg), or 4 percent, were tropical oils.

Michael Sumichrast, an economist and publisher of a construction newsletter, said that history could well repeat about ...

resented a sharp re from the original re world trade, and the eff suppliers such as Mal would likewise be minor

It was the first time ing activity has shown weakness since just be the last recession in 1981- promising to

Sigh. What are these guys doing?

GEICO gets a new boss, John Byrne

I'm going to kick ass!

Byrne knows he has to make drastic changes.

Are you saying there is no way that New Jersey will allow us to raise rates in the state?

Despite everything I have said?

Here's your !*X)#!! license! We're pulling out of New Jersey!

You government bureaucrats make me sick!

There's no need to...

87

We have to tell the 300,000 policyholders in New Jersey to get their insurance elsewhere.

Mr. Byrne, there's a call from Washington D.C.

Who the hell is it?

It's the regulator. He's saying he'll shut us down unless we can reinsure some of our risks.

GNASH

Oh, great! Just great!

Mr. Buffett, it seems you have powerful friends.

I'm told I have to agree to meet you.

GEICO's looking like the Titanic.

I can't let it collapse. It was my first big stockpicking success.

And Lorimer Davidson was so good to me when I went down there as a dumb student...

And Ben Graham still owns a lot of GEICO stock.

Warren arranges a meeting with John Byrne.

So, how do you plan to save the company?

I'm cutting the workforce in half...

89

They talk long into the night.

From what you say, GEICO still has a big cost advantage over its competitors.

Sure, if we can ever dig ourselves out of this hole...

GEICO only spends around 15% of its premiums on overheads. The industry average is 24%. The basic business is still sound...

91

Byrne persuaded other insurance companies to take the rest of the reinsurance...	But only if GEICO raised new capital **WHAT?**	I need you to underwrite a stock issue!

But Wall Street firms didn't want to know... *GROAN*	I don't think there's anywhere else to go We're finished

This is our last chance.

Salomon Brothers.

I can't say I like them much.

Byrne had been invited there to talk to an analyst.

The number two boss had agreed to see him afterwards.

Hello, Mr. Gutfreund.

PUFF

PUFF

I don't know who you think is going to buy your !*%^! reinsurance deal.

John Gutfreund was famous for his tough-guy act.

You don't know what you're !*%^! talking about.

At least he has balls.

You look at these numbers. You help us now, and you'll make a bundle.

Soon...

It's worth saving GEICO.

And Warren Buffett is buying — he has already invested $4 million.

Hmmm

He's even taken some of the reinsurance, and he's trying to smooth things with the regulators.

Sounds like Buffett is serious.

I'll talk to Buffett.

We'll never persuade the other firms to take a piece of this.

Salomon's ass will be on the line!

Warren promises Gutfreund that he'll buy any unsold stock.

GEICO successfully raises $76 million in the new stock issue.

Within six months, GEICO's stock price quadruples.

BUFFETT'S RULE FOR SUCCESS No4

GIVE HELP AND ADVICE IF THEY WANT IT, BUT LET THE MANAGERS MAKE THEIR OWN DECISIONS.

In 1983, Warren gets interested in a local Omaha company, Nebraska Furniture Mart.

It's Omaha's biggest furniture store; in fact, it is the largest furniture store under one roof in the entire USA.

Putt
Putt

It is owned by "Mrs B.", who is 90 years old. She's a little ...outspoken.

Hey, get that stuff outta the aisle, you dummy!

What's the matter with you?

Lazy! You worthless golem!

Excuse me, Mrs B.

Who are you?

I'm Warren Buffett.

I'm interested in buying your store.

98

99

"Mrs B." was born Rose Gorelick in 1893 in Minsk, Russia.
She never went to school. Life was hard.
By the time she was 16, she was running a store in Minsk with 5 employees.
At 21, she married Isadore Blumkin. Russia was in chaos, and her husband decided to emigrate to the US. Rose was supposed to follow later.

In 1917 the revolution and the war with Germany made it almost impossible to get out.
Rose took the train to the Chinese border, then crossed Manchuria and made it to Japan - all without a passport.

Finally, she got to Seattle and was reunited with Isadore. They settled in Omaha in 1919. In 1937, Mrs. B set up a furniture store. Her motto was **"Sell cheap and tell the truth."**

Mrs B. could hardly speak English, let alone read and write it. It was almost impossible for her to borrow money.
She did the only thing she could do: increase turnover by keeping margins ultra-low.
Her average gross profit was only 10%.
Everyone in Omaha bought from Mrs. B....

CHAPTER 9 BUFFETT SAVES SALOMON BROTHERS

1991 Berkshire Hathaway has become a massive company but not that many people on Wall Street know Buffett well.

He likes to avoid the limelight.

Mr. Buffett, you have a call from John Gutfreund from Salomon Brothers.

Thanks.

I wonder what he wants.

SCRAPE

munch
munch

John
has
integrity,
but...

...Salomon
is still paying
its people
way too
much.

Everyone on Wall
Street gets
these crazy
bonuses.
They don't
deserve it.

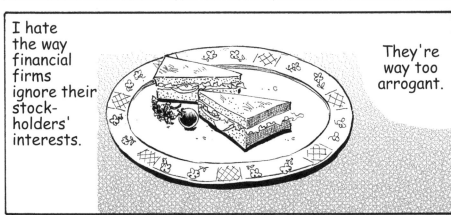

I hate
the way
financial
firms
ignore their
stock-
holders'
interests.

They're
way too
arrogant.

I have
invested
$700 million
in Salomon
preferred
stock. I get
9% a year
interest on
that, and
it's mostly
tax-free...

I can convert it to
common stock any
time before the end
of October, 1995 if
the price tops $38.

I wouldn't
lose much if
Salomon was
liquidated.

Wall Street despises its stockholders. It's obsessed by the short term. And a lot of people are flouting the law...

BUFFETT'S RULE FOR SUCCESS No5

NEVER, EVER BREAK THE LAW.

Salomon's problems were getting worse...

New York

ALOMON BROTHERS

Mr. Gutfreund, I have reached the Federal Reserve for you.

This is Gerald Corrigan.

Hello

Look, we have discovered that one of our employees has been making fraudulent bids for Treasury bonds, using clients' names without their knowledge...

When did you find out?

Well, we heard about one of them 3 months ago. But it now seems that there have been more.

Gutfreund had delayed for too long...

CLICK

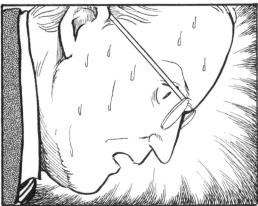

How the hell did this happen?

That trader was insane. What a goof! Damn! We could lose our license!

That guy is delusional. He has lied and lied and lied.

Now it makes me look guilty too!

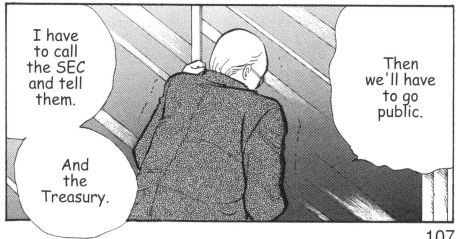

I have to call the SEC and tell them.

Then we'll have to go public.

And the Treasury.

We have enemies... They're going to have a field day.

Cigar-chomping Gutfreund was feared throughout Wall Street...

Gutfreund issues a press release...

The Wall Street Journal

SALOMON BROTHERS IN ILLEGAL TRADES!

mmending reduced the Malaysian Palm Oil dietary fats, espe- Growers Council has mounted rated fats. an information campaign and and cameras — and has underwritten medical stu- the in- dies to support its case. vious trial, a judge 095 that

The article implicates Gutfreund personally in the fraud.

This will bury me.

Omaha

DRRRINGGG!

Hi, it's John. I have to quit — everyone's gunning for me.

Would you come to New York?

I don't know, John. I need to think about it.

I don't want to get entangled in all this banker nonsense!

PAD PAD PAD

SWISSHHHHH!

SCRUB

PLOOOOOSH

This firm has $150 billion in assets, but only $4 billion is equity. Its liabilities are staggering.

...but it does have a franchise.

SHICKA SHICKA

Salomon's business is fine; it makes real money.

This is a management crisis — the bosses are being removed.

PLUF PLUF

They want me to take over as a caretaker CEO.

Investment banking is about confidence...

No one thinks I'm a city slicker.

I'd look good — a clean pair of hands.

Charlie Munger thinks the whole idea is insanely risky; Buffett's reputation could be totally destroyed.

Even Buffett's son, Howard, warns him against it, arguing that he is making himself a target for anyone who has a grudge against him.

Warren can't resist trying to save the day...

Salomon Brothers,
New York

We are in deep, deep doo-doo.

They'll retrench me first, I know it.

Gutfreund has to go.

Who is this Buffett guy?

He'll slash the staff by 75%; what does he care?

I heard he thinks we make too much money.

Hey!

Who's that old guy?

He doesn't look like an investment banker. Maybe he's from the Treasury.

113

115

Warren summons a meeting of all the managers.

As you all know, I have resigned. We're extremely lucky that Warren Buffett has agreed to step in as interim CEO.

Thank you, John. I know we're all stunned and saddened at this turn of events.

Salomon Brothers has broken the rules. We are under criminal as well as civil investigations. The Fed, the SEC, the Treasury and many other agencies are out to get us.

From now on, we have to be whiter than white. We will adhere strictly to every regulation.

Anything near the line, not only on the line, will be called out.

Salomon only has a future if it can keep its investment banking licenses. We have to send a clear message that there will be no more funny business.

CLAP CLAP CLAP

Okay, John, let's go and see the Fed.

OK.

Warren, they're pissed. You're going to have to...

I'll be appropriately contrite on our behalf.

117

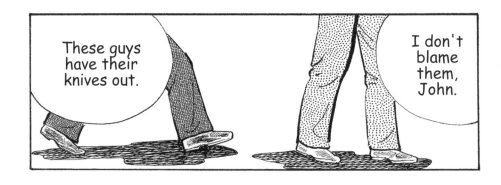

These guys have their knives out.

I don't blame them, John.

At the Federal Reserve...

Gerald Corrigan

I want to see sweeping reforms at Salomon, Mr. Buffett. Its entire corporate culture is suspect. If you don't fix it, I'll put it out of business permanently.

Hmm

118

Mr. Corrigan, I will do everything I can.

I'm sure it can be done.

That could have been worse, I guess.

I don't blame the regulators for being so mad.

I'm mad too.

The next morning, Buffett calls the top executives to a meeting.

One of you is going to have to be the next boss. Come into the next room one at a time, and tell me who you think it should be.

A friend arrives...

Hiya, hotshot!

Charlie!

Am I glad to see you!

How bad is it?

Bad, Charlie, real bad.

We're facing potentially huge fines, loss of licenses, criminal charges...

and more importantly, our credit lines could easily dry up any time.

I'm going to need your legal expertise.

This is the toughest one ever, Charlie.

The next day Buffett holds another board meeting.

Over here for the camera!

Please let me through.

Mr. Buffett!

DROOM

SLAM!

ARDR

PANT

I'm sorry to inter-rupt...

The Treasury has just suspended our right to participate in their bond auctions! They want to speak to you, Warren.

GASP!

He doesn't care if Salomon goes under. You'd better draw up the bankruptcy papers just in case.

Right away.

Look at the time!

The Tokyo market will open soon.

I have to get the government to give some sign of approval as soon as possible.

It's Charlie Munger to see you sir.

Squeak

Okay.

Warren, don't become CEO!

You don't have to.

This mess isn't your fault.

If things get worse, you could get personally banned from stock trading.

Thanks a lot, Charlie.

That's a big help.

What are friends for?

John has resigned,

and I've instituted a raft of controls.

Good.

I think I was little hasty earlier.

I'll allow Salomon to participate in the bond auctions,

but only on its own account, not for customers. That should give the markets a positive signal.

I really appreciate this.

Let's see if he can do it...

The board meeting finally ends, and a press conference is called.

CLICK

SNAP

WHIRRR

I have agreed to step in as interim chairman. Deryck Maughan here will manage Salomon.

I'm stun- ned.

I'll try to answer your questions in the manner of someone who has never met a lawyer.

Ho ho

I don't know all the details myself, yet,

but I'll do my best to explain what's going on.

Have you read Liar's Poker?*

Yes, I did read it a while ago.

Any comment on the book?

I hope there won't be another edition!

* *Liar's Poker*, by Michael Lewis, painted an ugly picture of Salomon's trading practices.

Mr. Buffett!

Warren!

My turn!

I have to make them see we're changing.

There have been inexplicable and inexcusable failures of management.

It's my task to root out all the causes and ensure that Salomon never breaks the rules again.

The press conference goes well. Warren heads back for another meeting.

Deryck is in charge from now on. He'll hire and fire.

So don't call me, call him.

I'll be doing my best to keep the regulators at bay.

It's up to you people to clean up your act.

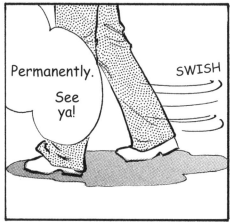

Permanently.

See ya!

SWISH

That's all?

THUNK.

Well, that's decisive.

We know what to do now.

The next day

We just lost a customer - California Public Employees' Pension Fund.

Connec-ticut and Massa-chusetts too.

The World Bank has pulled out.

Have we got leprosy?

Everyone hates us now.

Our debt rating has been downgraded.

That figures.

Buffett and Munger visit the Securities and Exchange Commission (SEC).

WHISTLE

I'm gonna press for criminal charges.

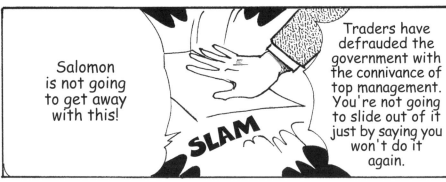

Salomon is not going to get away with this!

SLAM

Traders have defrauded the government with the connivance of top management. You're not going to slide out of it just by saying you won't do it again.

Does he know something we don't?

We can't afford to be prosecuted.

We should fire Salomon's lawyers.

Cut all the bonuses.

Warren, if Salomon is prosecuted, it doesn't matter if it wins or loses.

The damage will be terrible.

All we can do is 'fess up.

They'll turn this into a circus.

You know what these high profile cases are like.

Uncle Sam loves a scapegoat.

Being open is our only chance, Charlie.

BUFFETT'S RULE FOR SUCCESS No6

OWNERS ARE OWNERS AND MANAGERS ARE MANAGERS — BUT THEY SHOULD WORK AS PARTNERS.

In September there's a congressional hearing.

chatter   rustle

I want to start.

Buffett takes the stand.

...by apologizing...

The nation has the right to expect its rules and laws will be obeyed.

You hear that?

No one on Wall Street ever apologizes!

136

137

hush

The SEC ask to see a confidential report on the fraud from Salomon's lawyers.

We're under no legal obligation to give them this.

It will be extremely damaging if they get hold of it.

I don't want to hear all this lawyer talk.

We did wrong.

But...

We're going to admit to everything.

And take our punishment.

I'm going to keep my promise to be open. And we're going to stop using all these political advisors.

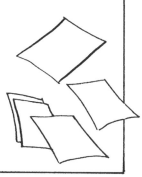

Buffett orders Salomon to stop dealing with Marc Rich, the fugitive oil trader.

He halts all gifts to political parties.

Mr. Buffett, all our best people are resigning.

PLOP

The press is turning against you.

I'm doing what I think is right.

Everything is turning sour.

The media say Buffett is out of his element and has lost his touch.

At the U.S. Attorney's office

We want Salomon to plead guilty to a felony and pay a fine of $400 million.

How long are you going to be...

...associated with the company, Mr. Buffett?

Warren is sick and tired of Salomon. He's upset that so many people have defected. But soon there's good news.

There will be no prosecution and the fine is reduced to $290 million.

Salomon's stock price rises.

He said he'd finished what he had to do.

Did you know he didn't receive any salary?

Wow.

Well, I guess he can afford not to be paid.

A rich guy like that.

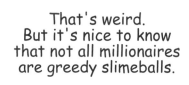

That's weird.
But it's nice to know
that not all millionaires
are greedy slimeballs.

BUFFETT'S RULE FOR SUCCESS No7

KEEP YOUR DISTANCE FROM THE MARKET.
YOU'LL UNDERSTAND THE BUSINESS BETTER!

Was Buffett's adventure with Salomon a mistake? For many years, a lot of people thought so. The huge bonuses were gradually reinstated and many of his reforms ebbed away.

Warren had the last laugh in 1997, when Traveler's Insurance Co. acquired Salomon Brothers for $9 billion with Warren's blessing — his own shareholding was now worth $1.7 billion.

In the following year, Citigroup merged with Travelers. Warren slowly began to sell his stock. He had reduced his holding in Citigroup to only $110 million, and, ten years later, he held no stock at all.

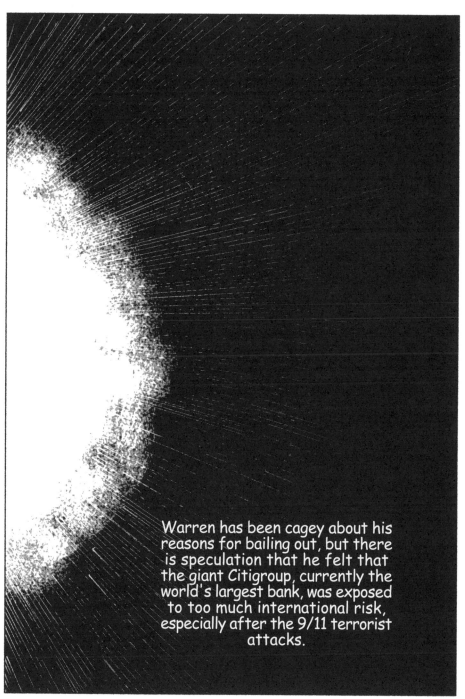

Warren has been cagey about his reasons for bailing out, but there is speculation that he felt that the giant Citigroup, currently the world's largest bank, was exposed to too much international risk, especially after the 9/11 terrorist attacks.

CHAPTER 10 BACK HOME

It's good to be back.

I did not enjoy that at all.

I'm better suited to the quiet life.

What was I thinking? I must have been nuts.

149

A few years back, the Reds were in deep financial trouble.

Warren bailed them out.

That's why everyone around here loves him.

People were really moved by what he said then.

I remember.

I want people to feel proud of their local businesses.

What a guy!

Do you have any Berkshire stock?

Every year, thousands of people flock to Omaha for Berkshire Hathaway's AGM.

A lot of them come to see a ball game.

Where are you from?

Ja-pan

You own Berk-shire stock?

Yep.

So do I.

I only bought one B share so I could come to the meetings.

Same here.

Do you think...

...we're being groupies?

Who cares? I just like his attitude.

You wanna check out the Nebraska Furniture Mart?

Yeah. Then I want to drive past his house.

More than 10,000 people descend on Omaha each year for the meeting. It's like a Star Trek convention.

People seem to want to relive the American Dream, back the way it was in the 1950s, when people had morals and didn't lock their doors...

Over here!

Mr. Buffett!

Will you give me an auto-graph?

Mr. Buffett, I lie awake at night worrying what will happen if you pass away.

So do I!

HA HA HA

I'm not kid-ding!

Actually, Warren has made careful plans for Berkshire's future after his demise.

I've reached the age when you think about your past.

I'm basically an introvert...

who enjoys simple pleasures.

I have been lucky enough to find a way to use my talents fully.

Could I have made it as a normal company executive?

I doubt it.

APPENDIX CHRONOLOGY

Year	Age	Rank	Capital (US$)	Event
1877				Washington Post founded
1886				Coca-Cola founded
1888				Hathaway Manufacturing Co. founded
1889				Berkshire Cotton Manufacturing Co.
1893				Mrs. B (Rose Blumkin) born
1921				See's Candies established
1929				Stock Market Crashes, Great Depression begins
1930				Warren Buffett, first child of Howard and Leila Buffet, is born
1936	6			GEICO is established
1937	7			Nebraska Furniture Mart established with investment of $5 million
1940	10			National Indemnity established
1943	13			Buffett begins delivering newspapers
1946	16			Enters Wharton School and University of Pennsylvania
1949	19			Meets Benjamin Graham, author of *The Intelligent Investor*
1950	20			Graduates from U. of Nebraska
1951	21			Graduates from Columbia U. School of Business Enters employment of "Buffett Falk & Co."
1952	22			Marries Susan, buys $10,000 of GEICO stock
1953	23			Sells GEICO shares for $15,000
1954	24			Enters Graham's company Graham-Newman
1955	25			Berkshire Hathaway is founded
1956	26			Graham retired Berkshire Associates is founded (Capital of $105,000)
1962	32			Partnership is reorganized Acquires shares in Berkshire Hathaway
1963	33			Buffett's fund becomes Berkshire's leading shareholder Katharine Graham becomes president of *the Washington Post*
1964	34			Acquires shares of American Express
1965	35			Operating capital grows to $26 million Assumes control of Berkshire by holding 49% of shares Acquires shares in Walt Disney Enterprises
1967	37			Buys National Indemnity and National Fire & Marine for $8.6 million
1969	39			Buffett personally owns 29% of Berkshire Partnership is dissolved
1972	42			Buys See's Candies
1973	43			Acquires 10% of Washington Post Co.
1974	44			Made a director of Washington Post Co.
1976	46			Acquires part ownership of GEICO
1977	47			Buys the Buffalo News

Year	Age	Rank	Value	Events
1982	52	82	$250M	
1982	53	23	$520M	Acquires 80% of Nebraska Furniture Mart
				Blue Chip Stamps becomes wholly owned subsidiary
1984	54		$660M	
1985	55	23	$170M	Berkshire's existing textile operation closes
				Acquires Capital Cities/ABC shares
1986	56	5	$1.4B	Buys Scott Fetzer
1987	57	7	$2.1B	Buys convertible-preferred stock shares
				in Salomon Brothers
1988	58	9	$2.3B	Acquires Coca-Cola shares
				Acquires Freddy Mac shares
1989	59	2	$4.2B	Acquires preferred shares in Gillette
				Buys Borsheim's Fine Jewelry
1990	60	2	$3.3B	Buys Wells Fargo Bank shares
1991	61	4	$4.2B	Salomon Brothers illegal trading incident
				Buys H.H. Brown Shoe Co.
1992	62	4	$4.3B	Buys Lowell Shoe Co.
1993	63	1	$8.3B	Buys Dexter Shoe Co.
1994	64	2	$4.2B	
1995	65	2	$12.0B	Sells Capital Cities/ABC shares
				Sells Helzberg Diamonds
				Buys R.C. Willy Home Furnishings
1996	66	2	$15.0B	Buys McDonald's shares
				GEICO becomes fully owned subsidiary
				Buys Flight Safety
				Issues Berkshire Class B shares
				(value of 1/30 of Class A shares)
1997	67	2	$21.0B	Sells McDonald's shares
				Buys Star Furniture
1998	68	2	$29.4B	Invests in silver, buys Executive Jet
				Buys International Dairy Queen
				Mrs. B dies at age of 104
1999	69	3	$31.0B	Buys Walt Disney shares
				Buys Jordans Furniture
2000	70	4	$28.0B	Sells Freddy Mac shares
				Buys Mid American Agency
				Buys Coat Business Services
				under the name Wesco Financial
				Buys U.S. Liability
				Buys Justin Industries
2001	71	2	$33.2B	Buys Shaw Industries
				Buys Benjamin Moore
				Buys Johns Manville
				Buys Mitec
				Buys XTRA Corporation
				Acquires shares in Moody's, H&R Block
2002	72	2	$36.0B	Buys Albecca
				Buys Fruit of the Loom
				Buys Gallant
				Buys CBT Int'l Corp.
				Buys Pampered Chef
2003	73	2	$36.0B	Buys Clayton Homes

* Ranking according to Forbes 400

BIBLIOGRAPHY

Buffett: The Making of an American Capitalist, by Roger Lowenstein. Japanese translation by K.K. Business Bank, Sogo Horei Shuppan, 1998.

Winning Buffett's Way (Buffett de katsu -- anato no shisan unyo no tame ni), by Tetsu Emori. Sogo Horei Shuppan, Feb. 2000.

The Warren Buffett Way: Investment Strategies of the World's Greatest Investor by Robert G. Hagstrom, John Wiley & Sons. Translated by Atsuo Mihara and Ichiro Ono, Diamond-sha, 2001.

Damn Right: Behind the Scenes With Berkshire Hathaway Billionaire Charlie Munger by Janet Lowe. John Wiley, 1999.

Buffett -- the Man Who Moves "U.S.A. Inc." (Buffett, "Beikoku Kabushiki Kaisha" wo ugokasu otoko) by Hiroshi Makino, Nihon Keizai Shimbun-sha, 1999.

Buffettology Work Book by Mary Buffett and David Clark. Translated by Tadasuke Idei and Yasukazu Nakaguma, Nihon Keizai Shimbun-sha, 2002.

The Essays of Warren Buffett: Lessons for Investors and Managers (Wiley Finance) translation supervised by Atsuhiro Doko, Kazumi Masuzawa and Miyo Niimi 2002 (Panrolling).

Investment Planning Manga/In the Shadow of the World's Top Investor, Buffett, by Janet Lowe. Translated by Kazumi Masuzawa, others, 2001 (Panrolling).

The Warren Buffett CEO: Secrets from the Berkshire Hathaway Managers by Robert P. Miles. Translated by Noriko Kimura, 2003 (Panrolling).

Of Permanent Value: The Story of Warren Buffett by Andrew Kilpatrick (Birmingham) htt://www.berkshirehathaway.com/.

Wizard: Lessons from the Legends of Wall Street by Nicky Ross. Translated by Noriko Kimura, 2001 (Panrolling).

Where to go for investment success.

Warren Buffett

0-470-82078-0
February 2002

WARREN BUFFETT SPEAKS

Wit and Wisdom from the WORLD'S GREATEST INVESTOR
JANET LOWE

0-471-16996-X
March 1997

WARREN BUFFETT WEALTH

Principles and Practical Methods Used by the World's Greatest Investor

ROBERT P. MILES

0-471-46511-9
March 2003

FROM THE BESTSELLING AUTHOR OF THE WARREN BUFFETT WAY

ROBERT G. HAGSTROM

The Essential BUFFETT

TIMELESS PRINCIPLES FOR THE NEW ECONOMY

FOREWORD BY BILL MILLER, LEGG MASON VALUE TRUST FUND

0-471-22703-X
August 2002

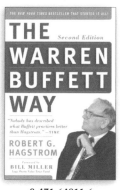

THE NEW YORK TIMES BESTSELLER THAT STARTED IT ALL

THE WARREN BUFFETT WAY

Second Edition

"Nobody has described what Buffett practices better than Hagstrom." —TIME

ROBERT G. HAGSTROM

Foreword by BILL MILLER

0-471-64811-6
October 2004

"Simply the most important new stock book of the 1990s, its date. Buy it and read it." —Kenneth L. Fisher, FORBES

FOREWORD BY PETER LYNCH

Worldwide Bestseller

The WARREN BUFFETT WAY

Investment Strategies of the World's Greatest Investor

ROBERT G. HAGSTROM, JR.

0-471-17750-4
March 1997

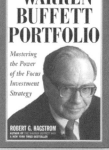

BUSINESS WEEK BESTSELLER

The WARREN BUFFETT PORTFOLIO

Mastering the Power of the Focus Investment Strategy

ROBERT G. HAGSTROM
AUTHOR OF THE WARREN BUFFETT WAY
A NEW YORK TIMES BESTSELLER

0-471-39264-2
November 2000

"Your book is terrific. It contains helpful advice and is easy to read." —WARREN BUFFETT

What I Learned Before I Sold to Warren Buffett

AN ENTREPRENEUR'S GUIDE TO DEVELOPING A HIGHLY SUCCESSFUL COMPANY

BARNETT C. HELZBERG, JR.
Former CEO of Helzberg Diamonds

0-471-27114-4
March 2003

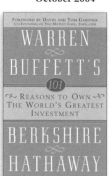

FOREWORD BY DAVID AND TOM GARDNER
Co-Founders of The Motley Fool, Fool.com

WARREN BUFFETT'S 101

REASONS TO OWN THE WORLD'S GREATEST INVESTMENT

BERKSHIRE HATHAWAY

ROBERT P. MILES

0-471-43046-3
April 2003

"EVERYONE KNOWS WARREN IS THE GREATEST INVESTOR OF OUR TIME. . . . THIS BOOK FOR THE FIRST TIME CAPTURES HIS GENIUS AS A MANAGER." —JACK WELCH

THE WARREN BUFFETT

SECRETS FROM THE BERKSHIRE HATHAWAY MANAGERS

CEO

ROBERT P. MILES

0-471-43045-5
April 2003

DAMN RIGHT!

BEHIND THE SCENES WITH BERKSHIRE HATHAWAY BILLIONAIRE CHARLIE MUNGER

JANET LOWE
FOREWORD BY WARREN BUFFETT

0-471-44691-2
May 2003

WILEY

Now you know.

wiley.com